D1572862

How to Write a Memoir

by Nel Yomtov

CHERRY LAKE PUBLISHING • ANN ARBOR, MICHIGAN

CHERRY LAKE
Publishing

Published in the United States of America by Cherry Lake Publishing
Ann Arbor, Michigan
www.cherrylakepublishing.com

Content Adviser: Gail Dickinson, PhD, Associate Professor, Old Dominion University, Norfolk, Virginia

Photo Credits: Page 4, ©Noam Armonn/Shutterstock, Inc.; page 7, ©Tadas_Naujokaitis78/Shutterstock, Inc.; page 14, ©Naypong/ Shutterstock, Inc.; page 15, ©Elena Elisseeva/Dreamstime.com; page 16, ©Rob Marmion/Shutterstock, Inc.; page 19, ©Photoeuphoria/ Dreamstime.com

Library of Congress Cataloging-in-Publication Data
Yomtov, Nelson.
  How to write a memoir / by Nel Yomtov.
    pages cm. — (Language Arts Explorer Junior)
  Includes bibliographical references and index.
  ISBN 978-1-62431-188-8 (lib. bdg.) — ISBN 978-1-62431-254-0 (e-book) — ISBN 978-1-62431-320-2 (pbk.)
  1. Autobiography—Authorship—Juvenile literature. I. Title.

  CT25.Y66 2013
  808.06'692—dc23   2013008074

Cherry Lake Publishing would like to acknowledge the work of The Partnership for 21st Century Skills. Please visit www.p21.org for more information.

Printed in the United States of America
Corporate Graphics, Inc.
July 2013
CLFA13

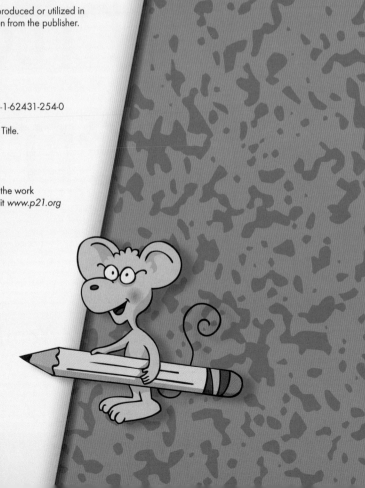

Table of Contents

CHAPTER ONE

Your Stories Are Important!

Your relatives probably have many interesting stories and photos to share.

Think about the times your relatives have told you stories about the past. Maybe they've told you about the way things were when they were growing up. Perhaps they told you about special events that shaped their lives. You may be young, but you have many stories to share with others.

One way you can share your stories is by writing a memoir. A memoir is an **account** of your personal experiences. You can write a memoir about your entire life. You could also just write about certain parts of it. You don't have to be famous to write a memoir. You don't have to be old either. Anyone can write a memoir!

Writing your memoir can be a lot of fun. Reliving your most important experiences can be enjoyable. You might even learn a few things about yourself. And once you write your own life story, you'll be proud of the many good things you've accomplished. Let's get started!

CHAPTER TWO

What Makes a Good Personal Story?

A memoir is like any good story. It needs three basic parts. These parts are characters, settings, and an interesting plot. You should also mix in some **conflict**. Maybe you could include a story about a time you got in trouble at school. A little humor and even some sadness will make your stories more interesting.

Your memoir should also have a good plot. The plot of your memoir is the action and the events that make up your life. You might write about moving to a new town. You could describe what it is like to change schools and make new friends.

Your memoir can tell stories about your favorite memories with your pets.

You already know the main character in your memoir. It's you! You have many memories of your life. Think about your first friend or the first family trip you took. You also know all the feelings inside you. You know your hopes, dreams, and fears. Other characters in your memoir can include your relatives and friends. You could even write about your pets!

Settings are the locations of your story. They could include your school or even your entire town. Don't forget places you've visited or stores you went to.

Reviewing a Story

You are getting ready to write your own memoir. It is often helpful to think back on stories other people have told you. In this activity, you will describe what it was like to listen to someone else tell a story about his or her life. The story can come from anyone, including a relative or a friend.

HERE'S WHAT YOU'LL NEED:
- Pencil
- Ruler
- Notebook paper

INSTRUCTIONS:
1. Write the name of the storyteller and the subject of his or her story at the top of a sheet of paper.
2. Use a ruler to help you make three boxes.
3. Look at how the boxes in the chart on page 9 are labeled. Label your chart in the same way. Each box is for a different idea.
4. Fill in the boxes of your chart with your thoughts about the experience you had with your storyteller.

To get a copy of this activity, visit www.cherrylakepublishing.com/activities.

Sample Storyteller Review Chart

STORYTELLER'S NAME: Grandpa Sherman

SUBJECT OF STORY: Working at a newspaper

WHAT MADE THE STORY MEMORABLE:

- Interesting characters, such as Grandpa's boss, Frank Adams
- The setting of the newspaper office. It was always busy, and the workers enjoyed the fast pace of their jobs.
- The way Grandpa told the story. He described the setting in detail and used things people actually said.

WAS HE OR SHE A GOOD STORYTELLER?

- Grandpa was excited to tell his story. He was funny and liked sharing part of his life with me.
- He got me involved in his story and made me feel almost like I was with him working in the office.
- When he told me sad parts of his story, he showed he cared about the other characters.

WHICH OF HIS OR HER STORYTELLING SKILLS DO I HAVE?

- I give lots of details about people and places when I tell a story.
- I can tell a story with lots of emotion to make it interesting.
- I like sharing parts of my life with others.

CHAPTER THREE

Brainstorm!

Where do you get the material that you'll need to tell your life story? You simply begin by jogging your memory. Do some creative brainstorming! Here are a few suggestions:

Make "memory lists." Make two lists. The first is a long list of things from your past. Think about people you've met and places you've visited. Recall events you have attended. Include anything you can think of. Even include things that seem unimportant.

The next list should include only the most important events or relationships that have shaped your life. Your life would be very different without these events or people. Limit this list to about eight items.

Gather family stories. Make a list of family stories that you've heard from older relatives, especially if you're one of the characters in the story. Write down people's names and where they lived. Try to remember the jobs they held and as many other details as you can.

Collect important items from your life. Fill a box with things that bring back special memories. These things could include a photo of you as a young child or your first baseball cap. They could also include a favorite toy or anything else that has been important to you.

Look through family photo albums. Who are the people in the photos? Do you know them? How? Are you in any of the photos? Where were the photos taken? What were you doing there?

Make Lists

You will make two memory lists in this activity. One will be a long list of people, places, events, thoughts, or feelings. The second list will be major events in your life that shaped who you are.

HERE'S WHAT YOU'LL NEED:
- Pencil
- Ruler
- Notebook paper

INSTRUCTIONS:
1. Use a ruler to help you make two columns.
2. Write "Memory Lists" at the top of the page.
3. Write "Long List" at the top of the left-hand column. Write "Major Events" at the top of the right-hand column.
4. Fill in the chart with your personal memories.

To get a copy of this activity, visit www.cherrylakepublishing.com/activities.

Memory Lists

Long List
- My seventh birthday party
- First baseball game
- Brother Bill broke his leg
- Trip to New York City
- First airplane model
- Hiking with Mom
- Our first cat, Podges
- Visit to dentist
- Joined Cub Scouts
- First day in preschool
- Playdate with Matt

Major Events
- Moved to Florida
- Grandma passed away
- Birth of my new sister

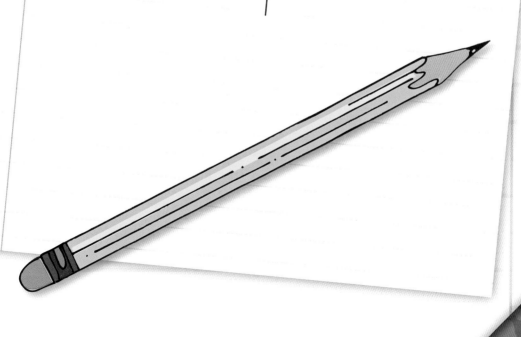

CHAPTER FOUR

Make Your Story Come Alive!

Start by writing about your most interesting memories.

It's time to turn your memories into an exciting written story. Choose a few memories you most want to write about. Don't worry if you leave some out. You can always add them later! You can begin your memoir by describing the very beginning of your life.

But you can also start with a joke or even a shocking fact about your life.

Start each new memory on a separate sheet of notebook paper. You can also type your memories on a computer. You'll organize each memory later to make a full-length memoir. Write many short stories instead of one long story. Describing huge chunks of your life might be difficult. It is much easier to write a little bit about each event in your life.

A computer can make it easier to rearrange memories into a different order or add new details.

Use details to create a mood. Carefully describe the characters and settings of each memory. How did something taste and look? How did it sound and feel? How did someone speak? What unusual habits do your characters have? Adding details will help your stories mean as much to your readers as they do to you.

A story about your birthday might include details about how the cake tasted or who came to the party.

ACTIVITY

Practice Writing

Details and action words help bring writing to life. This activity will help you learn to make your memoir interesting. The paragraph below is from a young boy's memoir. Read it carefully. How would you rewrite the story to better describe the people, places, and action? Rewrite the story using stronger descriptive words and action words to create a more interesting memory.

To get a copy of this activity, visit www.cherrylakepublishing.com/activities.

Sample Memoir Story

My dad took me to my first baseball game on June 24. We drove to the stadium. Then we bought tickets and took our seats. We sat close to the playing field. The New York Mets were playing the San Francisco Giants. The weather was good. The grass had just been cut. It smelled nice. The first San Francisco batter swung and missed at the first pitch. Then he hit a long fly ball into the stands for a home run. The crowd cheered.

CHAPTER FIVE

Putting It All Together

Have you written the stories you want to include in your memoir? Good! Now it's time to organize them. Put together your memories to create a larger picture of your life story. Here are a few different ways to do this:

Organize by time. You could put your earliest childhood memory first in your story. Then you would place stories from your kindergarten years. These would be followed by first grade stories, and so on. Organizing your stories by time is an easy way for people to follow your memoir.

Organize by subject. If you organize your memoir by subject, you might put everything about school in one chapter.

Stories about your parents could go in a separate chapter. Vacation stories would be placed in yet another chapter.

Organize by theme. A **theme** is the main idea of a piece of writing. If you've written stories about your parents, some themes might include love, friendship, or disappointment.

Now that you've got your stories organized in some way, you have to link them together into one long life story. You can do this by

How will you organize your memoir?

writing short phrases to connect them. Simple phrases you can use include, "Another thing that happened was . . ." or "He also said . . ." or "Another time . . ."

After you are done writing, read through your memoir. Are your characters, settings, and actions described in detail? Do the connections between the stories make sense? Are your stories interesting to other people? It may be necessary to rewrite parts of your memoir to make it the best you can make it.

By writing your memoir, you've explored your life and the lives of people who you care most about. You've taken the first exciting step in discovering yourself!

STOP! DON'T WRITE IN THE BOOK!

ACTIVITY

Edit Your Memoir

Ask yourself these questions as you reread your memoir:

☐ YES ☐ NO Are the names of people and their relationships to me clear?

☐ YES ☐ NO Is it clear where and when the memories took place?

☐ YES ☐ NO Have I described characters, settings, and actions with enough detail?

☐ YES ☐ NO Are all words in my memoir spelled correctly?

☐ YES ☐ NO Have I used correct punctuation throughout my memoir?

☐ YES ☐ NO Have I grouped similar memories together into longer sections?

☐ YES ☐ NO Do the connections between the individual stories make sense?

☐ YES ☐ NO Have I used dialogue throughout my memoir?

Glossary

account (uh-KOUNT) a description of something that has happened

conflict (KAHN-flikt) a struggle or disagreement

memoir (MEM-wahr) an account of an author's personal experiences

plot (PLAHT) the main story of a memoir or a work of fiction

theme (THEEM) the main subject or idea of a piece of writing

For More Information

BOOKS

Kalman, Bobbie. *I Can Write a Book about My Life*. New York: Crabtree Publishing, 2012.

Kamberg, Mary-Lane. *The I Love to Write Book: Ideas & Tips for Young Writers*. Milwaukee, WI: Crickhollow Books, 2008.

WEB SITES

Creative Writing Now—How to Write a Memoir
www.creative-writing-now.com/how-to-write-a-memoir.html
For advice on how to write a memoir, as well as interviews and ideas to inspire your memoir writing.

TIME for Kids—Writing Tips
www.timeforkids.com/homework-helper/writing-tips
Check out some useful tips that will help you complete any writing project.

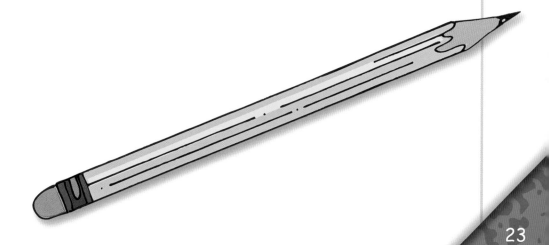

Index

About the Author

Nel Yomtov is an award-winning author of nonfiction books and graphic novels for young readers. He lives in the New York City area.